TRUE STORY OF A CHILDHOOD TAKING AWAY
THE STORY TELLS YOU OF MY LIFE
GROWING UP IN THE SOUTH EAST OF IRELAND

LIKE A LITTLE GEM OF THE WORLD

WHERE IT SHOULD BE FILLED WITH LOVE AND JOY

NOT LIES ABUSE DANGER   NO CHILD SHOULD
HAVE TO LIVE LIKE THIS NOT NOW NOT EVER

DONT SUFFER IN SILENCE LIKE I ONCE DID THERE

IS HELP WAITING ...

i would like to take the time to
thank my wonderful husband
james for always been by

myside every step of the way
and my sister mary brother in
law noel and also my sister
rose and brother in law
stephen and my in laws the
Hogan family here and in uk
thank you for sticking by me
and believe n in me and not
giving up on me and a huge
thank you to my councillor
nuala i can never thank you
enough

you showed me to believe in
myself and showed me i was
not mad and it was not my
fault i will be for ever greatfull
to you and most importaint i
am normal thank you all xxx

the view of river
from the woods
above our home

SUNNY SOUTH EAST,,

I lived in a little village called knockanore . it was
a nice quiet place to live in co waterford . the
sunny south east as it was called to us.   our
household was made up by my dad and mam.
and then there was nine girls me and my sisters.
growing up back then was very different to these
days. our house was a small three bedroomed but

all that. we needed then with large sitting room kitchen and bathroom looking back now I think how did we all. manage to fit in there but we did our house was down the end of a country road all around it was fields as far as the eye could see it was beautiful the woods we use to walk in and the river blackwater was not far from our house just a short walk down the bog as we used to call it true the woods and you would be there; we could look across the river bank andountry the village was small but had.

everything you need from day to day in country life it had a shop post office church school not to forget at the time two pubs so we only needed a trip to the big towns maybe once or twice a week and they would be tallow or Dungarvan I was the youngest of the nine girls we were split in two are groups there was the five older girls and the four youngest I oftened wondered how my mam was able for us all but she had help I was told from my older sisters to help with us small ones mam was a quiet lady always had a smile on her face even when sometimes she didn't want to she was always cooking or doing something around the house then there was my father he was always wheeling and dealing in something from horses to cars

my confimation day

you name it dad would try and make money from it but he didn't like to share his money with mam it would be kept to buy another money making thing he was always doing something with cars and tractors in the big shed he had just up from our home house mind you to me it was full of rubbish but to him he knew where every part of car ect I was the youngest of the nine girls and I loved my mam and dad life was good it was normal to me some of my older sister as time went by moved out got married and started their new life but at that time I was as happy at home

I loved to be out and about with whatever horses or donkeys my father would have around the place mind you they never stayed for long no matter if you had a bond with them money talks and they would be gone just like that we had a sheep dog called spot he was the best he followed us kids everywhere been the youngest I was treated quiet well if I asked for something nine times out of ten I got it but I see my sisters been treated different sometimes my father was quiet strict with them but I didn't know any different .

THINGS WERE ABOUT TO CHANGE ....
it would have been around the late 80s I would
have been about seven years old I'll take you back
to 84 I was six and anyone who knew me knew
my love for animals didn't matter what type or
kind but my one true love was horses and pony's I
remember my father saying to me if I be good I'll
get you a pony there was a horse fair coming up in

8

the next few months it was held every year it was
a big event in tallow people came from all over
the country trying to make a sale on the day or
buy a nice cob or pony the weeks passed the fair
day was coming closer

I was so excited as any child of that age would be
but as the days came closer I started to feel sick I
wasn't right mam took me to the doctor in the
health center and there he told her home to bed
that I had chicken pocks I was so disappointed all
this time counting down the days and now mam
said I couldn't go now I know she was right but
back then telling a six year old kid you can't go
was like the world was ending the day had come
dad was up early as always mam in kitchen
cooking dad said by I thought that was it I wasn't
going to get anything now cause I know what dad
was like he would forget about it cause he would
see something else the day passed so slow it was
coming close to the evening and nothing but then

a car and my father's voice he came down to the
room and told me to go to look out the window I

was so happy I looked out my mother's bedroom window and there they was one black as coal pony with a white star on her head and there was a few donkeys but I was so happy dad had got her for me I named her dolly and this was the day my life would change for ever and not for the better as the days went by I was feeling a lot better I couldn't wait to get out that door to go out with dolly dad told me I had to take care of her so I did

I use to brush her for ages with this what was called a curry comb it must have been about ten years old falling apart but I didn't care dad would come out and show me how to take care of her from cleaning her feet to just leading her around till I got use to her he was like any normal father helping his child making memories but that didn't last long .

mam and me
loved her always

THE GREEN SHED ..

right next to our house in our garden there was a
shed we called it the green shed mind you it was
nothing to look at it was old and dirty my father
was not one for keeping things tidy I remember
there was a small grey box on it think my mam
had it there for birds so I use to bring dolly in to
brush her and one day my father came in and
asked me how I was getting on with dolly I said
quiet excited really good I would spend time just
doing her hair I just loved her when dad entered
the green shed to see how I was getting on he
pushed passed me I didn't know any different I
thought he was looking for something as he kept
stuff everywhere but even at that young age I
know I didn't like it I knew it wasn't right this kept
happing   a lot when I would take dolly in there I
could smell the dirty oil from his clothes he was
that near to me this continued so

I   didn't want to use the green shed anymore for
dolly how could someone you trusted and loved
could do that to you make you feel like that even
at such a young age my dad was always my hero
when I was little he abused his trust he know the

12

damage he was doing but that never bothered him not one bit .both my mam and dad I seen them fight I remember I could see what now I know to be fear in my mother's eyes she couldn't fight back she was small lady but she always said don't worry it will be ok i know now that my mother was not happy with him but back then i guess you made your choice so you had to live with it you would never leave your husband no matter what and she didnt she stayed by his side till the very last day of her life even after everything .

SCHOOL TIME ..
true my primary school days I had two best friends who I am still friends with to this day we use to take it in turns every weekend to go to each other's houses it was great I got to escape what was going on at home   even if it was only for a few hours on a Sunday my friend who live just up the road from us her dad had horses to he was

such a gentleman he was so different to my father he use to take us round the field on the horses and he was always smiling we would spend ages sitting out colouring and playing games thren her her mam would make us hot chocolate it was great fun my other friend lived just a tiny more bit up from her house

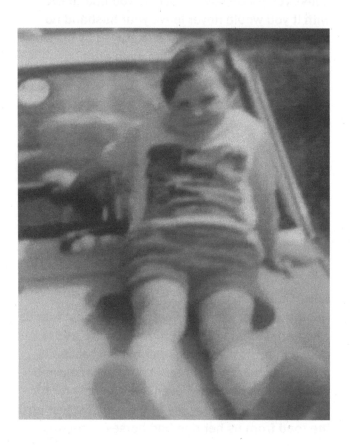

we use to go for long bike trips three of us were
always never far from each other we use to have
great times I remember there was a huge tree in
the yard in knockanore school and our parents
use to park behind the wall there I remember
seen my friends jumping in to their cars happy out
big smiles on their faces happy to see their
parents and happy to go home I wasn't if I could I
would of stayed in school all day long cause I
knew the car journey home was not going to be
good it was tainted unless the odd time mam was
in the car if she needed the shop I hated going In
the car with my dad the abuse started to happen
in the car on the way home from school never on
the way I was so scared of that small trip home it
felt like for ever but why was my father doing this

to me what had I don't to deserve to be treated in
such a bad way .this continued it   was like a part
of everyday life I blocked it out from a very young

child I wished it would stop I wished to be normal he was a great man for blackmailing you he used to say he would get rid of dolly mind you I didn't care by now i didnt want her anymore cause i know what would happen but it wasnt dollys fault either she was a pony but she was mine but

in a world of
my   own

he had taking my love for her away as I now knew

been round dolly something bad would happen
but then he would say if you tell your mother she
will go and I didn't want to be left with him down
there in that house in the middle of nowhere I do
remember my mam leaving a few times but she
took us kids with her she would leave and head
for my grandmother's house nan lived in Lismore
town   she lived on her own my grandad had died
in 1981 mam was her only child that still lived
nearby the rest had left for the big city lights of
Dublin the north and Uk to build new life's for
them self's   and they did pity my mam

 didn't get the chance to break free   from him
but how could she nine children in tow but my nan
was a very strong woman and she was a good
judge of crater she never liked my father at all
and she was right not to but we would no sooner
get to Nannys house when he would be in to take
us all home again it was a never ending circle   he

knew what he was doing to my mam the mental
abuse alone i dont know how she kept going .i
only wished my mam was strong to leave him and
we could of stayed with my nan he wouldnt dare

17

cross nanny i think deep down mam would of left
if she didnt have so many kids but we will never
know now .

SAVING GRACE ..
when my oldest sister toni got married, she had a
daughter   that they named grace she was five
years younger than me but we were very close we
would spend lots of time with each other she was
like the little sister I never had dad use to play the
good grandfather he would go and visit my sister

most days to pop in for a chat see the grandkids
and bring them sweets or biscuits like any good

grandparent would do I loved when I got to stay
there overnight we would play for hours on end we
got on really well we made jam with my sister we
were just left to be kids grace had to younger
brothers but we didn't bother with them we were
too busy playing house playing in the woods to
just sitting on the big green lawn at my sisters just
been with her we always had fun   I always
remember one day my father called down and
asked if grace wanted to come to nanny and
grandads house for a sleep over well I kicked up
and said I didn't want grace to come over and stay
my sister must of thought I was a right cow grace
was

the oldest grandchild but no I created such a fuss

19

I was told get in the car and shut up my sister
didn't let grace down over it all she must of
thought i was a really nasty child as she was
always so good to me thank god it had worked I
didn't want grace to be treated like I was I had to
protect her it's so cruel at such a young age I had
the fear he was going to hurt my grace even at a
young age i was not going to let that happen
grace was such a little doll blonde hair just perfect
in every way to me   my life was full of fear well
on the car trip home was I in for it I got a back
hander as he use to like to call it in to the face
and told never again to do that I cried he told me
shut the f==k up or there was plenty more from
where that came from so I

just sat there trying not to cry in case I got hit
again was this the life of a young child to have
getting up each single day living in fear at what
was going to come next I wished so many times I
was not here . as i look back now that poor child i
once was afraid to tell afraid to ask for help i was
truly dead from the inside out it got to the stage i
had no more tears left to cry my mind was black
to block out the here and now i didnt want it to be

the man i thought was my hero

THE FRIENDS ..

dad had a lot of different friends calling down all
the time for bits of tractors or cars and I didn't like
any of them I never felt comfortable when they
were around they would come in and drink tea
and chat for hours I just stayed out of the way to
be honest I didn't want to be anywhere near my
father I stuck to my mother in later years I found
out that some of his so called friends in the end

were convicted child abusers just like him you do
have to think to yourself did he know what they
were like and why would you have people like that
round your family home   I think my mother at
some point must of said cause she knew her
place if anyone called there was always tea and
cake put before them she was scared but I always
ask myself did mam know what was going on was
she afraid   I will never know now but i was told
mam said she had taking her marrage vows and
she would not break them but what do they really
mean he didnt love us he didnt love her he was a
nasty piece of work no marrage in this world

22

would keep me married if it ment keeping my children safe i know times were so different back then but really something could of been done but maybe she was afraid to ask for help and i know to well myself how easy it is to be in the place and been afraid so i never blame my mam for anything she had it just as bad but in a different way .

GETTING ON WITH NORMAL DAY TO DAY

over the course of time I tried to fit in as any
normal school kid I made my communion I
remember mam got me this lovely white dress
my father didn't go to stuff like that it was always
only my mam and I would see my friends in the
church with their mams and dads but never mine I
use to think was it my fault was it because but I
was lucky I still had my mam by my side I didn't
care I didn't want him there anyway he was taking
my childhood away from me making me feel like
a bit of dirt   I didn't do very good at school as you
can tell from the spelling mistakes in this book
but im not going to say sorry just another thing he
took from me school life

 I couldn't concentrate I was always thinking
about the hurt I was going to endure on the way
home I remember one day it was a either a
Thursday or Friday our good friends always came
to visit one night a week I use to look so forward
to see my friend jess and her mum and dad she
had two younger brothers   but when they use
to come down we would head outside and hang
out with the horses or donkeys we would chat for
hours she was a great friend and I loved her
coming down sometimes

I went round there house she loved animals also
she had the most amazing pet rats   o I loved
them we would take them out and play with them
and bath them all normal things kids should be
doing having fun my dad got to know them over
horses and donkeys but this evening my father
decided to go over to his other friend's house to
pick up something for his tractor so I had to go
with him cause I had to pick mam up milk on way
home so off we went when we got there   there
was only the farmer at home his family was gone
into town we sat down at the kitchen table they
had tea and they were chatting and about after
twenty mins dad stood up and I did to I thought it
was time for home but dad said to me sit down
there I won't be long I must just pick something
up in the yard I didn't think nothing of it but dads
friend didn't go with my dad he stayed in the
house with me he

me and mam

was always a nice man not like my dad I thought until that very evening my father had walked out that room and left me at the hands of another abuser did my father know ? I think is because he looked at his friend before   he left the room dad knew and he left me with that this very tall man pushed me down   pulled my bottoms   down and all I remember is the weight of him was crushing

my chest I couldn't breathe I wanted to die I felt pain like I never felt before it was like someone stabbing my insides the tears flowing down   my face how could they do this it's like they killed my soul that day   it was like it was going on for ever but in a matter of fact it was over in a short few mins but the damage was done he got up like if nothing ever happened and went out the door

I pulled on my bottoms the pain I couldn't hide I never cried so much in my life and with that my father shouted come on jack were going I got what I need I ran to the car as best I could I sat in the back and didn't say a word I couldn't get out the car at shop my father went in and he never would go in to any shop where we were nearly home he said you get in to the bath and sort yourself out when you get home and he said put

all of that in the bath water and he threw me a
box of Epson salts

   I said nothing but I did as he said as soon as the
car stopped off I went in to bathroom and had my
bath as I sat in the bath water I cried   the bath
water was bright red I was in bits   I was so sore I
was cut down below I sat there for ages my
mother shouted are you nearly ready for your
supper jackie I replied yes mam I'll be out now
soon I didn't want to come out the bathroom ever
again how could he do this to me and it not long
before my birthday and dad just walked into the
house like if nothing had even happened and sat
down in the sitting room and had his mug of tea i
oftened wondered was he right in the head its like
someone with a split mind how could he ....

   what had I ever done in my short life for this to
happen to me I really wanted to tell someone but I
didn't want my mam to go and leave me   he
knew what he was doing he was not stupid he
knew I wouldn't tell cause of mam over time mam
seen the marks on my legs she asked me i said i

got them from playing on the trees no more was said i really wish i could of told my mam or my friends i really do i was only a child but as i said before i was die n on the inside wishing someone could help but i couldnt speak out i really wish i had the currage to back then .

my father

WAS IT HAPPENING TO MY OTHER SIBLINGS !!!!
I really wanted to ask my other sisters did it
happen to them as well but no way would I but
taking you back to one cold frosty morning one of
my older sisters was to get up to catch the school
bus it just so happened she was the only one

31

going in for that day the other two was off sick she
woke me at seven thirty it was so cold cause there
was no heating in our house the inside of the
bedroom windows covered in frost and she said
will you please come in the car with me to the bus
stop as she said daddy won't touch you cause
you're the youngest how wrong was she I froze in
the bed

and I said no olive as I knew if I did what my faith
would be she never said another word about it
after that so I knew from that day it wasn't just
me why was he doing this to his children he is
meant to protect us all from people like him not
him be one I said to my dad one day after he did
it again to me I'm telling   I could see the look in
his eyes the anger that was building inside him he
was a small but well-built man he said if you do ill
break your mouth

I said no more that evening he said jack come
here we had wild kittens in the big shed I thought

he was calling me over them so off I went he said
look I have something to show you and with that
he picked up his blow torch and Ill never forget it
he picked up a plyers   and held a nail in it held
it to the heat and he said if you open your mouth
you will get more then this the next time and with
that he stuck it to my leg   the pain and with that
he caught me by the back of the head   slammed
my head on to his work bench and not alone he
has scared me from the inside out I was left with
a little dint on my forehead and a   mark on my
left leg from the top of the nail he was pure evil

he really was I still get reminded every day now
cause I still have them two scares he called
himself a father a father is there to love and
protect there kids like my friends dads i always
wished my friend up the road her dad was my dad
i would say i have more happy times to remember
up there then i had in my own home as a child
thats sad but very true .

HOLIDAYS IN DUNGARVAN .

**two of my oldest sisters moved to Dungarvan it
was a town we never really went to it had loads of
shops pubs people not like our little place there**

34

was lovely walks to go on the beach was only out
the road when I went down there, I made friends I
played out with other kids' life was so different
there I never wanted to come back

but I remember my first time going to stay with
my sisters they both had boyfriends but the fear
was in me about men I stuck to my sisters but
over time I got to know they were not like him that
monster back in scart I could be free I could be a
kid

it was a lovely summers day and my sister said
we would go to the beach so we packed a picnic
and her boyfriend said I'll be back in a min off up
to the music shop on o Connol street and he
came back with a radio   and battery's I thought
it was the best thing ever   it was the best day
when we got back we went to jrs for take away I
loved been with them they lived in Mary street but
soon moved to Bournville there I made many
friends

it was life a different life me and my friends we
sit for hours on gallows hill watching the day go by
there was no fear when i was down with my

sisters o how i wished they could of kept me it
was eating my father when i was down there he
didnt want me to go down now because he was
afraid if i would speak out but i couldnt cause i
knew he would kill me when i got home i looked
forward to every summer or every chance i got to
go stay with my sisters i was like a different child

but when i would go home all the questions
started where did you go did you speak to anyone
in other words did you tell .   the abuse carried on
until my early teens but i was getting older i was
fighting back but i didnt have to for long as he
stopped but the damage was done in my head i
was dirty useless had no reason to live .

THE REASON WHY ....

the reason he stopped i think cause it all came
out about the abuse he had done to another
family member he had done it he had split our
family up for every there was a huge divide in it
and it was all his fault .over few years he still said

37

he didnt do it i knew he had but i said nothing i
was just glad he didnt come near me ever again
over years he went to court my mother could not
handle the stress of it all she had a heart attack
late one evening

 i called the doctor in yougahl we took mam in
and i had to go to hospital with her he went home
to tell the rest of the family and they came up
later .mam spend three weeks in hospital and was
home for three weeks till the day she died on
good friday i will never forget that morning the
phone rang he was meeting some fella at youghal
bridge for part of car it was just me and mam at
home but mam passed away with me and toni by
her side the fear i had i would be living on my own
with him cause it was only me

and mam and him lived in scart everyone else had
left my sister molly came home from uk we were
very close after we put mam to rest in lismore we
were all back in scart my auntie was there she
was always so lovely but she was heading home
to the kings county we said our good bye but my

sister knew i didnt want to be

here with him on my own i didnt even have to say
anything she ran after my auntie and asked her to
take me with her and she did only for my auntie
and uncle and there family i had so much love
and support and thats what i needed at that time i
spend weeks up there i didnt want to go home but
the calls started i had to go back i hated it mam
died in april he sold our house in sep bought
another one it was like a shed my oldest sister
came and tryed to get me to go with them and a
social worker but he made me write a letter to say

i didnt want to go with them we moved to the
other house on the 12th sep 96 and he had his
next court date in october 96 it couldnt come fast
enough i think in his own head he was going to
get a slap on the wrist and told stop now but his
faith was sealed off we go up to the four courts
oct 96 he was giving nine years the tears from

some of my sisters when the judge read it out he
stumbled back in shock i was smiling inside he
was going away for nine years life was good i
didnt have to see him i didnt have to think asbout
it all i tryed to block it out but that was short lived

THE MENTAL ABUSE

and just when i thought things were getting better
the mental abuse started the house he had
bought was out in the country but on a main road
i had small house two bedrooms sitting room
bathroom and big garden and fields across the
road the neighbours was so lovely out there
always a hello i had my two dogs prince and bingo
and he had left me to mind three colt foals one
we called black banagher and i had my beautiful
pony sally she was chesnut with white blaze
probley the only pony he bought that was good
quality

i would spend the days out taking care of the
horses and going in to cappoquin on wednesday
evening was movie nite in one of the pubs great
crack i was in a happy place till word got out the

41

the house we bought now people didnt want us
living there casue of what he had done and i can
understand that but i was the one living there i
was just 18 but i might aswell been in that jail i
was been punished for his crimes for a whole year

i stayed awake all night and had some sleep in
the day they poisoned my dogs on me the horses i
had to sell cause they were leaving them out on
the main road at all hours as soon as dark nights
came i had people banging on my doors and
windows they wouldnt leave me along i had

enough i went to stay with my auntie when my
sisters found out the abuse my auntie recieved
telling her to send me home i had to mind the
house for daddy his house was the last thing on
my mind but they wouldnt give up if they were
that bothered why wouldnt they go out and mind
it not a hope cause two of them came out on
night to see what i was on about and when the
crap all started they went home and left me there
they didnt care one little bit i remember coming
home they didnt want me back cause i was there
sister they just didnt want the house empty they
never once asked me was i ok they didnt give a
care in the world like the night not very long after i
came home i had went to visit one family member
and it was like i wasnt wanted there the mental
abuse was really getting to me the sneaky talking
behind my back so i went and i tryed to take my
own life i took what tablets i could find i wanted to
be gone only for the cousin of my family member i
wouldnt be here today two of my sisters steped
over me when i had falling on to the hall ground i
remember her stepping over me saying im not
missing my night over her they knew i had taking
an over dose but the person that was there called
another sister and she took me to hospital to be
pumped out maybe it would of been better for
them if i was gone ..

home house
with green shed
in view

VISITS

when your abused you try and live your life as they
say a normal life but you have to ask yourself
what is normal normal to me was trying to block
out everything get on with life as best i could i
went to visit my father in the joy and it was always
like he made out he shouldnt be in there they the
sent him,

to the curragh prison it was called the vatican

because it was full of old men some priest all sex offenders the prison was locked in behind the army barracks but he soon learned if he kept his head down he was able to get a job he was left out to the main area to clean up he was ment to be in there for what he had done not for a holiday camp and after all that he only served three years i know three years for all he had done the laws in ireland needs to change they really do three years he walked free not a care in the world thinking he was always in the right he did no wrong

three years for taking people childhoods i would of spoke out sooner only i seen how my sister was treated by her own flesh and blood they going around ware n there rose tinted glasses he should never of been left out he should of been left there i kept my mouth closed no one knew what had happened to me i carried on as best i could and to be far i did i blocked it out as best i could as they say out of sight out of mind my heart broke for my other sister it was wrong he only servied three years she is living a life sentance everyday for the rest of her life and i hated him for that not alone what he did to me but what he had done to her but yet he always came out thinking he was the best thing ever he had alot to answer for he really

45

had the hurt the pain the lifes lost all because of
him the sick twisted pedophile he was .

COMING HOME

he wasnt long out of prison and he has a new
woman yes i know right she moved in soon after
they fought like cat and dog i didnt get on with her
she was from wexford she had a bed and
breakfast down there she use to stay with him but
she ended up buying a house in lismore town but
in the end she passed away from cancer

i use to see him going shopping with her taking
her on holidays and he wouldnt help my mam,he
would do nothing to help her with nothing at all
even when he took her to town for the shopping
she had to pay him that in itself

nasty taking your wife to town to get the weekly
food shop and charge her .he soon got back to his
normal life it was like he was never inside he
started back at his car boot sales wheeling and
dealing had these people forgot what he had
done ?????????

what he had put his family true it was like nothing
ever happened my husband didnt know of any

47

what had happened to me i didnt want anyone to know to be honest i wanted to be normal but for years i really thought

i was mental that i was going to have a breakdown but my james was always there for me he was ands still is my rock . we visited my dad trying to have a normal life james would help him out with odd stuff taking him to pick up his car things like that buy now he has a new partner the other one had died and he soon replaced her this one was a nasty piece of work but i could only see good in her he found her on the mag like he found the other one in the lonely hearts page she wasnt long before she had moved down from drogheda she had family two sons she didnt speak to and few grandkids she was married but divorced he was an alcohlic mind you i couldny believe a word comes out her mouth i oftened thought to myself what kind of woman can move in with a convicted sex offender and share a bed with him after she knows what he did to his own kids i myself thinks thats very sick in itself she didnt care she had money by all accounts no one liked her at all very rude woman im sorry i can not call her a lady as she is far from it .

i was broking

i stopped going down i didnt want my girls down there i wanted them safe i remember one evening a few years after i stopped going down and i picked up the phone he answered and i said would you like to go for tea in the hotel and sort things out and his response to me was your dead to me and he hung up that just goes to show who was the better person i was willing to talk to give him a chance to put things right once and for all i thought for a min and i was so upset

i cryed in anger how dare he the man who took my childhood who put fear in me all my life did that he should be thanking me for giving him a chance i was so angery i called that number back before he could even say hello i told him everything i thought of him what he had done to me and how he split the family apart and then i hung up

i called my toni and told her and she said he is

evil and she was so right after that i didnt speak
to him for seven years i lived my life i was happy
he wasnt part of it

53

MELTDOWN

as time went on my girls were getting older and they wanted to be out with there friends it put pure fear in me they wanted sleep overs at there friends i wouldnt mind there friends staying here cause i knew they would be safe the abuse i had suffered as a child was now affecting my everyday life and it was putting fear in my head about how to protect my girls in a way they did suffer but i was trying to mind them as best i could i wouldnt let them down the strand with there friends as his house was down by it i hated saying no but i had to now they know and understand but at the time they didnt god love them i would of done anything to protect them they use always say mam why are you over protected with us now they know and i think they respect me for it they know why i was like that .

one of my sisters was sick and they sorted out a tea party at hotel in dungarvan we all went it was lovely you had the ones who was stuck up and my niece and myself we had a few drinks i was trying to hide the paib of what was going on in my head its like i was going to explode anytime soon and i did that night i lost it i ended up going to my sisters i didnt care how i got there i was going it was very late and i knocked on her door she let me in she knew she put her arms around me and took me in to the kitchen she made tea my brother in law got dressed and came up we all chatted she was sorry it had happened to me but as i said it wasnt her fault she couldnt have stopped it and my brother in law was upset he said i should of told him he said he would of killed him but when your told and its drilled in your head not to tell you dont they have in a way power over you and they miss use that power its like your a puppet on a string .

the hardest part was the nest day telling my husband i didnt want him to look at me any

different but i know he wouldnt he is a good man
always stands by myside always helps and
supports me in what ever i want to do he is my
rock and my best friend my soul mate i could
never be with out him when i told him he held me
and i knew everything would be ok . i still felt mad
at my father and some of my sisters james said

i should get some councling and i did the hardest
thing ever is to pick up that phone and ask for
help i called the number for waterford rape and
crisis number and chatted i to a lovely lady i can
never thank them for all they have done for me

then went to meetings you will never know how
much there support helped me in a way it was
easer to talk to some one i didnt know my
councilor is living proof how far i have come on
my journey that day i walked into my first meeting
i was a mess i didnt know my head i thought i was
mad i really did my mental health was not good
but over time and weeks of chatting i was getting
some where there was times i did want to not go i
made excuesses they were the days i didnt want
to think about what had happened to me i didnt
want to relive it i didnt want the nightmares back
in a way it was like i was looking true a window
looking at someone elses life that wasnt me it
couldnt be a damaged person but i now know i
was not the damaged person it was him the sick
and twisted pedophile

doing what i loved

as the year went on i knew in myself things were
getting better i was dealing with things so much

better i for the first time could look in the mirror and i could see who i really was with the depression of everything i had let myself go but that was when i didnt love myself i didnt care what i looked like i put on so much weight but i still smiled i looked a mess so i promised myself im going to find the real me who is inside waiting to come out now that i was in a better place with my mental health i could do this that little child who was locked away trapped in a sence inside me was going to be set free i owed it to her and myself he had taking to much of my life already even years after the abuse and the abuse i suffered from other members of the family but in there eyes they were never wrong ...

in time with the help of my councilor i tryed to get
back doing some things that had been taking
from me like horse riding i use to be good at it
how i got back at it was my youngest girl loved
horses and wanted to take up horse riding i said
of course i booked her in for lessons i went with
her every week at the start that fear was showing
its ugly head again so i found a lady she was just
the best so kind and care n i remember the first
time erin went i walked her up to the stables the
smell made me fell like getting sick it took me
back to that time in my life i had blocked out for
so many years the smell of the horses the hay
everything i could fell myself starting to panic as
soon as she was on that horse i moved away from
them and just watched her i could see the joy on
her face she was so good with them i was looking
at my child who i love and would do anything to
protect them seen her so happy i was happy i
thought to myself way was my father not just
happy to see me been happy with dolly overt the
weeks the kids started to learn to take care of the
ponys just like i had many years ago i would be
there watching her not letting her out of my sight i
knew she was safe but i couldnt leave her she
made me so proud she would often say mam stay
in the car there is no other mothers up here i
would just say i want to see how your doing and

62

that i was proud of her when she is older she will
know why mam was always there

st patricks day
with his girlfriend

but as the weeks went by i was trying to sort it in
my head he was the one who hurt me not the
horses i know he had taking yet another thing
away from me and it was my time to take it back
with both hands life was for living i was dead
inside for a long time and i was lucky to be here
so it was hard but i decided to give it one last try i
use to go up to the stables just to see the horses
when she had classes and getting use to it all
again and that day came we tacked up and i went

out with my daughter for a hack it was something
i never thought in a million years i would be able
to do this again and to share the moment with my
own daughter ment so much to me i had done it i
was angery for me not doing it sooner he had
taking it away from me for many many years but i
over came it all and i was back doing what i loved
so much

as time went by i had the support of my two
sisters toni and betty sometimes we were told if
he was sick or if he went to hospital to be far i
didnt care what was wrong with him what ever to
me he was welcome to it until one night late i got
a call from another sibling saying your not ment to
know but i think you should know father is in
hospital me and my others sisters that stood by
me were not ment to find out but you got to ask
yourself this question why whats the big deal not
as if i was going to go and visit him of course i
told my other two sisters they didnt care either
only ones who cared was his daughters who

minded him and protected him even thou he was
a pedo and probley one of the most dangerous
kinds this went on for months he was in and out
of hospital were were on a need to know bases
well when we were told he could of died that was
it who the hell do them siblings think they have
the right to take away from the rest of us to say
what we have to say before he leaves this world
he made it anyway i heard was back down in the
house with his partner from drogheda living the
life .

by all accounts my family members didnt like her
they had no time for her they said she was a gold
digger ???? they were watching out for there
inherentice but to be far i found out the hard way
she was one thing im not like them i have
learned you dont need stuff to remind you of
someone everyday of your life if they mean
something to you then you will hold there
memories close in your heart .most of the others
like to keep there loving memories close in there
wallets if its not green they dont see .

65

but one day i knew we would get that call to say
he was gone i was ok with that cause i had lost
my father years ago when he did that to me i had
done my crying hard as it may sound unless your
ever in this place you would never understand .the
lies and the secrets were still been spilled he was
addmitted to hospital we were told he was after
contracting covid 19 while in there we were told
he would never come out of there again only in a
box as my auntie was told but how wrong were
they he fought it and he got over it but you have to
ask yourself this question why was he still in
there ?????

she had gone off running back up home to her
family in drogheda to her ex daughter in law she
didnt care much for him when he was in hospital
she would have to put her hand in her own pocket
something she didnt like to do .... over weeks the

lies were still been told i spoke with toni and betty
and we said we will call the hospital the others
had told them not to tell us anything and if one
thing been his daughter now that im in a much
better place and stronger there was more then
one way to skin a cat as they say so i looked and i
got hold of his mobile number for someone who is
dieing he was well able to answer the phone ....

THE PHONE CALL ....

so i went down to my room for quiet and i dialed
that number my heart was racing what was i
doing and i was just about to hang up and he
answered i said hello he said hello i said do you
know who this is he said yes its jack my daughter i
said yes he then said you have not talked to me in
seven years i said yes and we know why and he
said yes i said why then he said i am sorry for
everything i haver done to you my heart sank he
said sorry for all he had done to me sorry was not
going ot cut it with me the damage was done but i
know im to soft and kind hearted before i could
say anything he was crying a eighty four year old
old man crying saying them b.;,.;s are leaving me

67

here to die i said why he didnt know he said he had nothing and he was hungery i didnt knowwas he lieing but im not heartless i felt sorry for him as i would anyone else in the same place he cryed down that phone like a child trapped no way out could i find it in my heart to help him yes i was not one bit like him in the way but i did say its not nice dad is it crying with no way out no one to turn to but i said i will help you ill try and find out whats going on and that i did i was getting no answers from hospital so i called him back i said ill be down in the morning to get answers the hospital was on lockdown because of covid 19 but that didnt stop me i went the next morning off i went and went round to where the out deparment was i told lady on door that my father was in med 7 for six weeks and i wanted to chat to his doctor they scanned me and left me in i didnt lie so off i went found where i was going and asked to see joseph dolan they said no well i said i am going no where till i see him with that harrold must of phoned the hospital for update to see if he was dead yet .

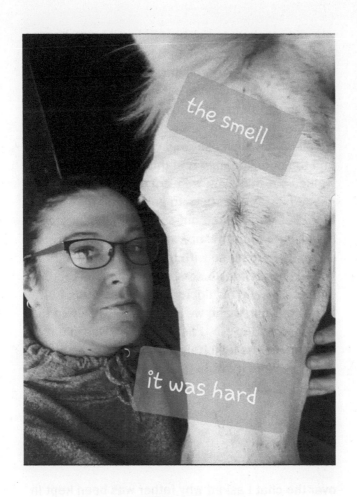

the smell

it was hard

and they must of told her i was there well the
phone started hopping what was i doing there o

why did i rock up to the hospital well i may have
not been in contact with him for my own reasons
but they forget he is still our father aswell how
dare they think they can cut us out if this was me
years ago i would of left it off but not this time the
nurse from the ward came out and said my father
would be out soon i sat and waited i looked up
and the doors opened and this small frail man
walked out mind you we were told by them he
needed 2 walking sticks to get around that was
more lies dad walked out crying he couldnt stop
he fell in to our arms he was just so happy to see
a family member so with that i said to the nurse i
wanted to see his doctors so they took us to a
small room and his doctors team was there and
head staff nurse and we chatted they listened to
what dad had to say i asked why he was in dirty
clothes and the hospital said thats what he had
and they were ment to be looking after there
father .

over the chat i asked why father was been kept in
the others had told the doctors that his partner
had gone back up the country and was now in a
care home which was lies yet again the doctors
told me about the large sum of money that was
taking from our fathers room in his house shortly

before 2.700 he had told the doctors they had robbied him blind was his own words they wanted to but him in a home and all he wanted to do was go home i said why are you holding him here its not right the doctors didnt know that harrold was not passing on info to me or toni or betty she had said she was the doctors didnt know any of this after all the others worked for the hse .

he trusted they were telling us the info of what was happening lets just say the doctors didnt like they were been lied to so they asked dad did he mind to put my name on his file as i was the one who turned up the others as the doctors said they taleded the talk but my point was my father was not stupid he remembered what he had done to me he said sorry he was not that far gone in the head he knew about his money that was taking they were making him out to be a prize fool so the doctors said dad could go home i told him i lived five mins aways and i would go up and down and check on him the others went mental that he was aloud home cause while dad was asways there was things taking from his house paper work ect and god knows what else just cause i was helping him i never forgave him and i never can my life could of been so different .

dad was home a few days happy out .when i got the phone call at 1.30 am from tilly

do you know your father is sleeping on the couch i said yes he wanted to its his choice he was watching tv

do you know your father is in a cold house .. that couldnt be as i left the heating on do you know your father is scared down there after this i hung up i didnt need to be listing to her crap i went down next morning he was fine happy out to be home he asked me and my niece to go and bring his partner back so off we went brought her back and shit was our thanks the other sisters didnt want to see her coming back they had one night the next morning tilly was down saying dad is very sick he needs hospital to me he was fine he knew i was mad i had just got him home why dont they leave him alone the ambulance came the guys were lovely they couldnt understand why they were called they checked him over he was fine but because of his age they took him in i walked him out to the ambulance i said a few days and you will be home that was the last time he walked out of his home they even had taking his right if he wanted to slip aways at home in his own house i will never understand why i really dont .

i had giving up i didnt care what i looked like

IN HOSPITAL

over the next few days they doctors said his
oxygyn was low but he was fine but then he went
down hill he gave up why wouldnt he when his
own tribe didnt care over next few days the doctor
called to come and say good bye off we went to
waterford i was not upset but i went i rang toni
and she followed me down to support me dad was
still awake but when they showed us to his room

toni was down at the car i was with his partner i
went in to this room and before me on the bed
was this very skinny man i said sorry thats not my
father im looking for joseph dolan she said this is
him the truth was after they had killed his spirit by
putting him back in hospital he gave up they
should be ashamed of what they had done he was
a mess of not eve n 3 stone in weight just there in
the bed i was shocked it couldnt be him i took his
hand i know it was him

cause he had a weird nail the way it would grow i
still didnt forgive him i said good by i told him toni
was with me and he asked for her as week as he
was toni was his oldest girl i went down and told
toni and she went up to him and said good bye
she didnt have to do it but she did we went home
expecting to get the call but no they called and
said if we wanted to go back down the saturday
we could so we took his partner down and we
stayed all they with her she was saying o joe your
going ot a beautiful garden where you will be a
beautiful rose in gods garden i said nothing but in

my mind you were going to the pitts of hell for what you had done to us but i didnt say anything i was been respectfull my niece emma was with us when we were about to go the nurse said one of us should stay it wasnt going to be long so i stayed emma couldnt and sally was to old to expect her to so they left and then it was just us he was in and out of sleep i had to put everything aside he didnt look like my father the evil man i had as a dad i sat there and i read a book then i would play all our irish music just to keep busy and to waist time i held his hand so he knew he was not on his own

next day a nurse came in and said the harrold was
here and she wanted me to leave the room i said
no im here with my father as i once was with my
mother i said there is no one stopping her coming
up i have nothing to say to her so harrold got on
the phone for back up saying i said she couldnt
come in and how upset she was tilly came down
to hold harrolds hand for the whole of five mins
they all dressesd in there ppe crap they shouldnt
have been on a covid ward cause they worked in
the community with the old people and they left
that hospital and went back to there jobs and toni
couldnt return to work with out getting test as she
worked in dungarvan hospital .

i was there with him the total of four nights i could
see by his face dad was afraid to cross over was it
because of what he had done on this earth who
really knows he passed aways the next night at 11

pm i thought it was finnaly over but that was far from it as they say the apple dont fall far from the tree the bullying and mental abuse was coming thick and strong from the others but i didnt let that get to me at all after i recieved the call he was gone i called and got his funeral sorted toni came with us and we made sure he had the best just cause dad had did that to me as a child i didnt have to be nasty it wasnt in me at all there was no respect showing at the funeral home the jokes and laugh n outside with the staff with harrold and others was not on it was not a school reunion . but what do you expect if they had left him to die on his own in the hospital they didnt care they couldnt leave him pass away in his own home as i think he wanted to do they took that from him toni and i tryed to give him that at least but it was not to be .after the funeral it didnt stop they gave his partner sally a nasty time in the end .

we had to put up cameras to make sure she was safe . they were linked to my phone after all she was a old woman . i didnt want anything to happen to her im not heartless. tilly left her a

77

nasty letter demanding fathers ashes when they came back from cork . they had it in there head that they were going to put some of his ashes on my mothers and sisters grave in lismore .you must think are they right in the head to even think of doing this . after what he did to my sister not to mind the years of abuse our mother had from him .well i was not going to let that happen as soon as his ashes came back . i took them back to my own home and kept him for nearly three months .so this would not happen i know my mother wouldnt have wanted dads ashes down in her grave think they forget i was the one living at home with the two of them . for a very long time and they hated each other i couldnt see no love there .

TAKING HIM HOME THE KINGS COUNTY .

father had always wanted to go back to his home town when he left this earth . he had always said it over the years i remember him saying it from a very young age .so thats what me and toni did . toni was there for me every step of the way . she didnt want to go to his funeral she is not a hyprocite . when she found out i had left to go to banagher . god love her she was on the road right behind me . i had arranged for fathers ashes to be buried in his beloved county he always wanted to be near his parents and brothers . and he was i had never buried ashes before i tell you it was hard . i had my husband my cousin and my wonderful auntie by my side it was quiet.

no mass father wouldnt have wanted that . after all the others had there good byes in cappoquin and cork . the man who done the grave he done such a wonderful job .father would of liked it . the others had it in there mind he was going to go in with our nanny and grandad . but see again it was not there call it was not there grave .my auntie made sure she put some of her brothers ashes in with there parents and brothers .and then we went and we put father to rest . where he wanted to be . to be far the others didnt want him to have a grave or headstone they wanted the cheap option .but toni and i said he would get the best he did wrong to me and i hated him for that .and i could never forgive him for any of it . but i didnt have to be heartless .he was still my father . the grave was ready as the man said it would be . he had told me what to do as i never as i said before

did this . i lowered his brass urn in to the grave as
we were told to .then we coved him over . his
partner played a song and we left . we had done
all we could for him . we took him home. he was
at peace now well so we thought .

SICK AND TWISTED .....

after we had finished we went to my aunties house for some tea and food .we were just chatting and i said to my cousins wife . will we go back and check the grave . i dont know i had a sick felling come over me .lucky the grave yard is only three mins from my aunties house . so off we went and to my dismay . i seen the flowers were pulled apart .my sinn fein colours taking away .but that wasnt all .they had dug his ashes up and reburied them how they thought he should be .i felt sick we could see the dirt was not how we left it . they had disturbed consecrated ground . how sick and they opened his urn like what did they really think we had put in there . to me this is a sick act and they are the ones who need help .and in the irish law its a criminal offence . but they thought the law dont apply to them . was this the right actions to take no .its sick and twisted . i called the garda they couldnt get over it .as i couldnt myself the garda came out from birr station . they had never had to deal with anything

as sick and as twisted as this before . you may
think what has this got to do about my story this
is to show what we are still putting up with . even
after his death

.next day the garda called us in to station in
banagher she was such a lovley lady and very help
full . they called one of my sisters and spoke to
her it was not olive . so who was it she informed
the garda of the others harrold and tilly and
harrolds husband was around banagher
yesterday . they had to be watching our every
move . my phone rang it was olive and i told her
what had happened and i told her the garda was
going to dig . him up again to finger print the urn
as i was the only one who had it and i buried
him .so after the call we went on about our day
the garda wasnt going to do that i just said that so
we could find out who done it .. and it worked a
treat the garda in banagher got a call from tilly
and very rude she was to the garda and she said
she did it . and it was her fathers grave and
what .and to her suprise the garda informed her

that the grave was owned .by her sisters toni and
myself .so it was up to us if we wanted to press
charges .i still think to this day it was a sick act to
do and the others who was there when she done it
are just as guilty to let that happen.

i was told it would be better if myself and toni
gave the grave over to the others .as father
wanted them to have everything . i spoke to toni
and you know what not a chance .we have what
they want and not all the money in the world will
get us to give the deeds over in there name .for
years i always thought i was the damaged one the
stupid one the worthless one .well im happy i am
the person i have become and its no thanks to my
parents .its thanks to myself i might not have
done my school years i may not have got the best
job in the world but im here and im proud of
myself and how far i have come and im truly
happy . i have three beautiful children and a
fantastic husband and my sisters toni and betty
life is good for me its very sad to go around and
think your better then anyone else .because i can

tell you now your not you came in to this world with nothing and you will go out the same .so be kind if you can and helpful . its funny really when he died you had people sending there condolence on R.I.P .IE . from school in the area just becasue may works there bet they didnt know they were writing it for probley one of ireland worse pedifiles .also the HSE where others work .

i still think what would of been my path in life . if i had come from a loving home .where would life have taking me . i will never know that now .but thats life .if you were lucky to have loving parents be thankful . its a gift thats not promised to all .i am just greatful i never gave up and i got help ,and i am where i am today in a good place just remember there is people out there who cares for each and everyone of you .it might not seem that way now but trust me if i can do it so can you all . just done let anyone silence you .they think they have the power to . no you have the power speak out .i one day picked up the phone

and i called dungarvan station about my father
this was every before he died . but i didnt have the
strenght to follow it true . cause i wasnt in a good
place .but im still on my journey in life and im
going to make every second of it count .we will all
have our bad days sometimes but now i smile
because i want to .not because i have to and you
can to i hope this will inspire people to seek help.

i will leave it there ....

but never forget ....

IM A SURVIVOR NOT A VICTIM .

Jacqueline Hogan .

RAPE AND CRISIS CENTER 1800 77 8888

SAFE IRELAND 090647 9078

CURA CRISIS PREGNANCY SUPPORT 1800 828 010

MENTAL HEALTH IRELAND 01 284 1166

S.H.I.P [SELF HARM INTERVENTION PROGRAMME0
087 2586028

SAMARITANS 116 123

NATIONAL COUNSELLING SERVICES 1800 234 118

EMERGENCY SERVICES 999 OR 112